PLEASE CONSIDER LEAVING A REVIEW ON
AMAZON IF YOU LIKED THIS BOOK!

Main Idea Clue Chaser

- What is the title of the text? This is usually the main idea.
- The introduction paragraph likely explains the main idea, and supporting details of the text.
- The main idea is what the text is mostly about.
- You can find out the main idea of a text by synthesizing the main idea of each paragraph.
- You can also determine the main idea of a paragraph by reading the first sentence.
- The main idea can sometimes be found in the last sentence of a paragraph.
- Supporting details help to explain the main idea.
- Ask yourself what the text is mostly about.
- Think about the five W's of the passage to summarize the text or find the main idea:
  - Who is the text/paragraph about?
  - What did you learn about them?
  - When did the events take place?
  - Where did the events take place?
  - Why did the events take place?

Day 1

- As you read, underline the main idea of each paragraph and circle two supporting details in the same paragraph.

The Bird's Journey

Bird migration is a captivating phenomenon that showcases the remarkable abilities of these winged creatures. Every year, millions of birds undertake long and arduous journeys, covering thousands of miles as they navigate across continents. This instinctual behavior is driven by the search for favorable conditions, such as breeding grounds, food sources, and suitable climates.

Migration patterns vary among bird species, but they generally fall into two categories: long-distance and short-distance migration. Long-distance migrants undertake epic journeys, spanning continents and often crossing oceans. These incredible travelers may fly over mountains, deserts, and vast bodies of water, relying on their innate navigational skills and environmental cues, such as the position of the sun and stars.

The reasons behind bird migration are diverse. Some birds migrate to breed in regions with abundant resources, while others escape harsh winters by seeking warmer climates. The changing seasons trigger a series of physiological and behavioral changes, preparing birds for their journeys. They undergo intense periods of feeding and fattening to build up energy reserves, which fuel their long flights.

During migration, birds face numerous challenges, including extreme weather conditions, predation, and human-made obstacles. Yet, their determination and adaptability allow them to overcome these obstacles. They fly in V-shaped formations or flocks, benefiting from the draft created by those ahead, conserving energy for the arduous journey ahead.

Bird migration also plays a vital role in ecosystems. It aids in the dispersal of seeds and nutrients, facilitates pollination, and influences species interactions. Many regions rely on the arrival of migratory birds for the balance of their ecosystems and the preservation of biodiversity.

Understanding and studying bird migration is crucial for conservation efforts. By tracking their routes and monitoring their populations, scientists gain insights into the health of habitats and the impacts of environmental changes. Protecting crucial stopover sites, creating safe flyways, and reducing human-made hazards, such as habitat destruction and pollution, are crucial steps to ensure the survival of migratory birds.

In conclusion, bird migration is a marvelous journey that showcases the resilience and adaptability of these remarkable creatures. It highlights the intricate connections between different habitats and emphasizes the importance of conservation efforts. As we witness the incredible feats of bird migration, let us appreciate and protect these magnificent travelers, ensuring their continued presence and the preservation of our natural world.

Day 2

- Review your main idea and supporting details annotations from day 1.
- Answer all of the questions on the following pages.

Which two of the following would make a great title for the text?

a. Bird's Travel for Fun
b. Bird Habitats
c. Migration, a Marvelous Adventure
d. Marvelous Pollinators
e. A Once in a Lifetime Journey
f. The Yearly Movement Patterns of Birds

Write your own title for the book.

_____

_____

_____

_____

_____

Questions

Who/what was the passage about?

_____

_____

What was the most important thing you learned about the "who"?

_____

_____

When does it take place?

_____

_____

Where does it take place?

_____

_____

Why/how does it happen?

_____

_____

In your own words, what is the main idea?

_____

_____

_____

_____

_____

_____

_____

_____

_____

_____

_____

Which three details best support the main idea?

a. Bird migration is a captivating phenomenon.

b. Bird habitats are important to their survival.

c. Birds disperse seeds and other things that are important to the earth.

d. Some birds migrate to breed in regions with abundant resources.

e. Reducing human made hazards will benifit birds.

f. Migration patterns vary among bird species.

Summarize the text in five sentences or less.

_____

_____

_____

_____

_____

_____

_____

_____

_____

_____

Main Idea Clue Chaser

- What is the title of the text? This is usually the main idea.
- You can also determine the main idea of a paragraph by reading the first sentence.
- The main idea can sometimes be found in the last sentence of a paragraph.
- You can find out the main idea of a text by synthesizing the main idea of each paragraph.
- Supporting details help to explain the main idea.
- The main idea is what the text is mostly about.
- The introduction paragraph likely explains the main idea, and supporting details of the text.
- Ask yourself what the text is mostly about.
- Think about the five W's of the passage to summarize the text or find the main idea:
  - Who is the text/paragraph about?
  - What did you learn about them?
  - When did the events take place?
  - Where did the events take place?
  - Why did the events take place?

Day 1

- As you read, underline the main idea of each paragraph and circle two supporting details in the same paragraph.

The Life Cycle of a Butterfly: A Marvel of Transformation

The life cycle of a butterfly is a remarkable journey of transformation, showcasing the wonders of nature. It begins with the egg, carefully laid by an adult butterfly on a suitable host plant. The tiny, often round, eggs are designed to protect and nourish the developing larva, or caterpillar, inside.

From the egg emerges the caterpillar, which is the second stage of the butterfly's life cycle. The caterpillar is voracious, consuming leaves and growing rapidly. As it eats, it sheds its outer skin in a process called molting, allowing it to grow larger. This stage is focused on feeding and storing energy for the next phase.

After several molts, the caterpillar enters the third stage, known as the pupa or chrysalis. Inside the chrysalis, the caterpillar undergoes a fascinating transformation. It releases enzymes that dissolve its body into a thick liquid, and from this liquid, the adult butterfly starts to form. This stage, called metamorphosis, is a time of profound change as the body reorganizes into the intricate structure of a butterfly.

Finally, the adult butterfly emerges from the chrysalis, unfolding its delicate wings. At first, the wings are soft and crumpled, but they gradually expand and harden. The butterfly must wait for its wings to dry and gain strength before taking its first flight. Once ready, it sets off on a journey to find food, mates, and suitable habitats.

The adult butterfly engages in essential activities, such as feeding on nectar and laying eggs. It plays a crucial role in pollination, transferring pollen from one flower to another, contributing to the reproduction of plants. The lifespan of an adult butterfly varies among species, with some living only a few days or weeks, while others may live several months.

The life cycle of a butterfly is a captivating example of nature's transformative power. From the tiny egg to the elegant adult butterfly, each stage holds unique wonders. By understanding and appreciating this cycle, we can deepen our connection to the natural world and gain a greater appreciation for the delicate and fleeting beauty of butterflies.

Day 2

- **Review your main idea and supporting details annotations from day 1.**
- **Answer all of the questions on the following pages.**

Which two of the following would make a great title for the text?

a. An Amazing Transformation
b. Cool Caterpillars
c. Moths vs Butterflies
d. Marvelous Pollinators
e. The Life of a Butterfly
f. Butterfly Eggs

Write your own title for the book.

_____

_____

_____

_____

_____

Questions

Who/what was the passage about?

_____

_____

What was the most important thing you learned about the "who"?

_____

_____

When does it take place?

_____

_____

Where does it take place?

_____

_____

Why/how does it happen?

_____

_____

In your own words, what is the main idea?

_____

_____

_____

_____

_____

_____

_____

_____

_____

_____

_____

_____

Which two details best support the main idea?

a. Butterflies have four stages in their life cycle.

b. Butterflies are important to the environment.

c. The adult butterfly emerges from the chrysalis.

d. Humans should help Butterflies when they can.

e. Each stages of a butterflies life is unique.

f. You should not touch a chrysalis.

Summarize the text in five sentences or less.

_____

_____

_____

_____

_____

_____

_____

_____

_____

_____

Main Idea Clue Chaser

- What is the title of the text? This is usually the main idea.
- You can also determine the main idea of a paragraph by reading the first sentence.
- The main idea can sometimes be found in the last sentence of a paragraph.
- You can find out the main idea of a text by synthesizing the main idea of each paragraph.
- Supporting details help to explain the main idea.
- The main idea is what the text is mostly about.
- The introduction paragraph likely explains the main idea, and supporting details of the text.
- Ask yourself what the text is mostly about.
- Think about the five W's of the passage to summarize the text or find the main idea:
    - Who is the text/paragraph about?
    - What did you learn about them?
    - When did the events take place?
    - Where did the events take place?
    - Why did the events take place?

Day 1

- As you read, underline the main idea of each paragraph and circle two supporting details in the same paragraph.

Fire Safety: Protecting Lives and Property

Fire safety is of utmost importance in our homes, workplaces, and public spaces. Being prepared and knowledgeable about fire prevention and safety measures can save lives and protect property. It is crucial to understand the potential hazards of fires and take proactive steps to prevent them.

Prevention is the first line of defense against fires. Ensure that smoke detectors are installed in every level of your home and test them regularly. Keep flammable materials away from heat sources and electrical appliances, and avoid overloading electrical outlets. Make sure to extinguish candles and smoking materials properly, never leaving them unattended. Educate yourself and your family on fire safety practices, including the proper use of fire extinguishers.

Having a well-thought-out escape plan is essential in the event of a fire. Create a plan that includes multiple exit routes from each room, and practice it with your family regularly. Designate a safe meeting point outside the house where everyone can gather after escaping. Teach children how to call emergency services and ensure they understand the importance of staying low to avoid smoke inhalation.

It is vital to equip your home with appropriate fire safety equipment. Fire extinguishers should be easily accessible and regularly inspected. Familiarize yourself with the different types of extinguishers and their specific uses. Install fire-resistant doors and windows, and consider investing in a fire sprinkler system for added protection. In case of a fire, quick action is crucial. If a fire occurs, remember to stay calm and call emergency services immediately. Alert everyone in the vicinity and evacuate the area following your escape plan. If your clothes catch fire, remember to "Stop, Drop, and Roll" to extinguish the flames. Never re-enter a burning building under any circumstances.

Fire safety is a responsibility that falls on every individual. By implementing preventive measures, creating escape plans, and staying vigilant, we can significantly reduce the risk of fires and protect ourselves, our loved ones, and our property. Stay informed, be prepared, and prioritize fire safety in your daily life.

Day 2

- Review your main idea and supporting details annotations from day 1.
- Answer all of the questions on the following pages.

Which two of the following would make a great title for the text?

a. Fire Safety 101

b. Fire Fighters at Work

c. Water Safety

d. Stop, Drop, and Roll

e. Protect Your Home From Fires

f. How to Escape a Fire

Write your own title for the book.

_____

_____

_____

_____

_____

Questions

Quick Note: some of the questions below may not need to be filled out. Complete this to the best of your ability.

Who/what was the passage about?

_____

_____

What was the most important thing you learned about the "who"?

_____

_____

When does it take place?

_____

_____

Where does it take place?

_____

_____

Why/how does it happen?

_____

_____

In your own words, what is the main idea?

_____

_____

_____

_____

_____

_____

_____

_____

_____

_____

_____

_____

_____

Which three details best support the main idea?

a. Prevention is the first line of defense against fires

b. Firefighters have an important job.

c. It may take time for fireifghters to get to a fire.

d. Police and firefighters work together to save lives.

e. It is vital to equip your home with appropriate fire safety equipment.

f. Having a well-thought-out escape plan is essential in the event of a fire.

Summarize the text in five sentences or less.

_____

_____

_____

_____

_____

_____

_____

_____

_____

_____

Main Idea Clue Chaser

- What is the title of the text? This is usually the main idea.
- You can also determine the main idea of a paragraph by reading the first sentence.
- The main idea can sometimes be found in the last sentence of a paragraph.
- You can find out the main idea of a text by synthesizing the main idea of each paragraph.
- Supporting details help to explain the main idea.
- The main idea is what the text is mostly about.
- The introduction paragraph likely explains the main idea, and supporting details of the text.
- Ask yourself what the text is mostly about.
- Think about the five W's of the passage to summarize the text or find the main idea:
  - Who is the text/paragraph about?
  - What did you learn about them?
  - When did the events take place?
  - Where did the events take place?
  - Why did the events take place?

Day 1

- As you read, underline the main idea of each paragraph and circle two supporting details in the same paragraph.

Pollinators: Nature's Vital Contributors

Pollinators play a crucial role in the reproduction and survival of countless plant species, making them essential for maintaining biodiversity and sustaining ecosystems. These remarkable creatures, ranging from bees and butterflies to birds and bats, facilitate the transfer of pollen from the male reproductive parts of flowers to the female parts, enabling fertilization and seed production.

Bees are among the most well-known and abundant pollinators. As they visit flowers in search of nectar and pollen, they unintentionally transfer pollen grains from one flower to another. Bees are particularly efficient and effective pollinators due to their fuzzy bodies that attract and carry a significant amount of pollen.

Butterflies, with their vibrant colors and delicate wings, also contribute significantly to pollination. As they flutter from flower to flower, they inadvertently transfer pollen while feeding on nectar. Butterflies are attracted to flowers with bright colors and strong fragrances, making them ideal partners in the pollination process.

Birds, such as hummingbirds, are prominent pollinators, especially in tropical regions. Their long beaks and specialized feeding habits allow them to reach the nectar deep within certain flowers, while pollen sticks to their feathers. As they move between flowers, these avian pollinators transfer pollen and aid in plant reproduction.

Bats, often overlooked as pollinators, play a crucial role in certain ecosystems. They are attracted to night-blooming flowers that emit strong scents and produce copious amounts of nectar. Bats have the ability to carry large amounts of pollen on their bodies and fur, ensuring efficient pollination of these specialized flowers.

The decline of pollinator populations is a matter of concern, as it can have far-reaching consequences for both natural ecosystems and agriculture. Factors such as habitat loss, pesticide use, climate change, and diseases contribute to their decline. To protect and support pollinators, it is essential to provide diverse and pesticide-free habitats, plant pollinator-friendly gardens with a variety of flowers, and raise awareness about their significance.

Pollinators are nature's vital contributors, playing a fundamental role in plant reproduction and the functioning of ecosystems. By understanding their importance and taking action to protect them, we can ensure the continued health and diversity of our natural world. Let us appreciate and conserve these fascinating creatures and the invaluable service they provide.

Day 2

- **Review your main idea and supporting details annotations from day 1.**
- **Answer all of the questions on the following pages.**

Which three of the following would make a great title for the text?

a. Birds, Bats, and Bees.

b. How Pollination Works

c. The Hummingbird

d. Marvelous Pollinators

e. The Animals of the Amazon

f. An Important Job

Write your own title for the book.

_____

_____

_____

_____

_____

Questions

Quick Note: some of the questions below may not need to be filled out.
Complete this to the best of your ability.

Who/what was the passage about?

_____

_____

What was the most important thing you learned about the "who"?

_____

_____

When does it take place?

_____

_____

Where does it take place?

_____

_____

Why/how does it happen?

_____

_____

In your own words, what is the main idea?

_____

_____

_____

_____

_____

_____

_____

_____

_____

_____

Which three details best support the main idea?

a. Pollen is important to the environment.

b. The Amazon is a place where many animals live.

c. Birds disperse seeds and other things that are important to the earth.

d. Butterflies have beautiful wings.

e. Pollenators are important to the environment.

f. Plants rely on Pollenators.

Summarize the text in five sentences or less.

_____

_____

_____

_____

_____

_____

_____

_____

_____

_____

_____

Main Idea Clue Chaser

- What is the title of the text? This is usually the main idea.
- You can also determine the main idea of a paragraph by reading the first sentence.
- The main idea can sometimes be found in the last sentence of a paragraph.
- You can find out the main idea of a text by synthesizing the main idea of each paragraph.
- Supporting details help to explain the main idea.
- The main idea is what the text is mostly about.
- The introduction paragraph likely explains the main idea, and supporting details of the text.
- Ask yourself what the text is mostly about.
- Think about the five W's of the passage to summarize the text or find the main idea:
    - Who is the text/paragraph about?
    - What did you learn about them?
    - When did the events take place?
    - Where did the events take place?
    - Why did the events take place?

Day 1

- As you read, underline the main idea of each paragraph and circle two supporting details in the same paragraph.

Climate and Weather: Understanding Nature's Dynamic Systems

Climate and weather are interconnected yet distinct elements that shape our planet's atmosphere. Weather refers to the day-to-day conditions in the atmosphere, including temperature, humidity, precipitation, and wind patterns. It is a dynamic and ever-changing system influenced by local and short-term factors such as air pressure systems and the movement of fronts.

Climate, on the other hand, refers to the long-term average weather patterns observed over a specific region or the entire planet. It takes into account factors such as temperature range, seasonal variations, and precipitation averages. Climate is shaped by various factors, including the Earth's rotation, the tilt of its axis, and the distribution of landmasses and oceans. It is also influenced by large-scale atmospheric patterns, such as El Niño and La Niña.

Understanding the difference between climate and weather is essential in comprehending the Earth's complex systems. While weather can change rapidly from day to day or even within hours, climate represents long-term trends and averages that span decades or centuries.

Climate change refers to significant alterations in long-term climate patterns, primarily driven by human activities such as the burning of fossil fuels and deforestation. It leads to shifts in temperature, precipitation patterns, and the frequency and intensity of extreme weather events. Rising global temperatures have far-reaching impacts on ecosystems, water resources, agriculture, and human societies.

Weather forecasting relies on meteorological data, sophisticated models, and satellite imagery to predict short-term weather patterns accurately. Meteorologists use this information to provide crucial forecasts, enabling communities to prepare for severe weather events, plan agricultural activities, and make informed decisions.

By studying climate and weather, scientists gain insights into Earth's intricate systems and the impacts of human actions. Efforts to mitigate climate change, adapt to changing weather patterns, and develop sustainable practices are crucial for safeguarding our planet's future. Understanding the dynamic relationship between climate and weather allows us to appreciate the complexity of our atmosphere and make informed decisions to protect our environment and communities.

Day 2

- Review your main idea and supporting details annotations from day 1.
- Answer all of the questions on the following pages.

Which two of the following would make a great title for the text?

a. The Weatherman
b. Climate Change
c. Dangerous Weather
d. Climate Vs Weather
e. Tornadoes, Storms, and Tsunamis
f. Learning the Difference between Climate and Weather

Write your own title for the book.

_____

_____

_____

_____

_____

Questions

Quick Note: some of the questions below may not need to be filled out.
Complete this to the best of your ability.

Who/what was the passage about?

_____

_____

What was the most important thing you learned about the "who"?

_____

_____

When does it take place?

_____

_____

Where does it take place?

_____

_____

Why/how does it happen?

_____

_____

In your own words, what is the main idea?

_____

_____

_____

_____

_____

_____

_____

_____

_____

_____

_____

_____

Which three details best support the main idea?

a. Humans should work to change the climate.

b. A weather person can predict the weather.

c. Climate and Weather are the same thing.

d. The weather refers to a short term pattern.

e. Climate and weather are interconnected yet distinct.

f. The climate is a long term pattern of weather.

Summarize the text in five sentences or less.

_____

_____

_____

_____

_____

_____

_____

_____

_____

_____

Main Idea Clue Chaser

- What is the title of the text? This is usually the main idea.
- You can also determine the main idea of a paragraph by reading the first sentence.
- The main idea can sometimes be found in the last sentence of a paragraph.
- You can find out the main idea of a text by synthesizing the main idea of each paragraph.
- Supporting details help to explain the main idea.
- The main idea is what the text is mostly about.
- The introduction paragraph likely explains the main idea, and supporting details of the text.
- Ask yourself what the text is mostly about.
- Think about the five W's of the passage to summarize the text or find the main idea:
  - Who is the text/paragraph about?
  - What did you learn about them?
  - When did the events take place?
  - Where did the events take place?
  - Why did the events take place?

Day 1

- As you read, underline the main idea of each paragraph and circle two supporting details in the same paragraph.

The Sun: Our Life-Sustaining Star

The sun, a blazing ball of gas at the center of our solar system, is not just a source of light and warmth; it plays numerous vital roles in sustaining life on our planet. From providing energy for photosynthesis to driving weather patterns, the sun's influence reaches far and wide.

One of the primary functions of the sun is to provide light and heat. Sunlight is essential for photosynthesis, the process by which plants convert sunlight into energy, releasing oxygen and supporting the entire food chain. Sunlight also helps regulate our sleep-wake cycles and promotes the production of Vitamin D in our bodies.

The sun's energy is the driving force behind our weather systems. Through a process called solar radiation, the sun's heat warms the Earth's surface, causing air to rise and creating atmospheric circulation. This circulation forms weather patterns, including winds, clouds, and precipitation. The sun's energy also powers the water cycle, evaporating water from oceans, lakes, and rivers, which eventually falls back to the Earth as rain or snow.

Solar energy is harnessed by humans as a renewable source of power. Through solar panels, sunlight is converted into electricity, offering a clean and sustainable alternative to fossil fuels. Solar energy is used to power homes, businesses, and even entire cities, reducing our dependence on non-renewable resources and lowering carbon emissions.

Furthermore, the sun plays a significant role in regulating the Earth's climate. Variations in solar radiation influence long-term climate patterns, such as ice ages and periods of warming. Scientists study solar activity and its impact on our climate to better understand natural climate cycles and to differentiate them from human-induced climate change.

In conclusion, the sun is much more than a celestial body that provides light and warmth. Its energy fuels life on Earth, enabling photosynthesis, driving weather patterns, and supporting the delicate balance of our planet's ecosystems. By appreciating the sun's multifaceted roles, we can better understand and preserve the intricate web of life that depends on its radiant energy.

Day 2

- Review your main idea and supporting details annotations from day 1.
- Answer all of the questions on the following pages.

Which two of the following would make a great title for the text?

a. The Stars of Every Galaxy
b. Our Star
c. Suns vs Stars
d. The Sun and Earth's Climate
e. The Sun and Our World
f. Solar Powered Lifestyle

Write your own title for the book.

_____

_____

_____

_____

_____

Questions

Quick Note: some of the questions below may not need to be filled out.
Complete this to the best of your ability.

Who/what was the passage about?

_____

_____

What was the most important thing you learned about the "who"?

_____

_____

When does it take place?

_____

_____

Where does it take place?

_____

_____

Why/how does it happen?

_____

_____

In your own words, what is the main idea?

_____

_____

_____

_____

_____

_____

_____

_____

_____

_____

Which details best support the main idea?

a. Our Sun is one of many in the galaxy.

b. A weather person can use the sun to predict the weather.

c. The sun is a red dwarf star..

d. Our solar system could survive without a sun.

e. The sun plays an important role in sustaining out lives on earth.

f. The sun's energy provides fuel for plants, dictates our weather, and can even be used to power electronics.

Summarize the text in five sentences or less.

_____

_____

_____

_____

_____

_____

_____

_____

_____

_____

_____

Main Idea Clue Chaser

- What is the title of the text? This is usually the main idea.
- You can also determine the main idea of a paragraph by reading the first sentence.
- The main idea can sometimes be found in the last sentence of a paragraph.
- You can find out the main idea of a text by synthesizing the main idea of each paragraph.
- Supporting details help to explain the main idea.
- The main idea is what the text is mostly about.
- The introduction paragraph likely explains the main idea, and supporting details of the text.
- Ask yourself what the text is mostly about.
- Think about the five W's of the passage to summarize the text or find the main idea:
    - Who is the text/paragraph about?
    - What did you learn about them?
    - When did the events take place?
    - Where did the events take place?
    - Why did the events take place?

Day 1

- As you read, underline the main idea of each paragraph and circle two supporting details in the same paragraph.

Egypt's Enduring Influence on the World

Egypt, with its ancient civilization and rich cultural heritage, has had a profound and enduring influence on the world throughout history. From advancements in architecture and engineering to developments in writing and mathematics, Egypt's contributions have left an indelible mark on various aspects of human civilization.

One of the most notable contributions of ancient Egypt is its architectural marvels, such as the Great Pyramids of Giza and the Temples of Luxor and Karnak. These awe-inspiring structures showcase the Egyptians' mastery of engineering and their ability to construct monumental and enduring buildings. The techniques and principles employed by the ancient Egyptians in their construction methods continue to inspire architects and builders to this day.

Egyptian hieroglyphs, one of the earliest forms of writing, have had a profound impact on the development of writing systems worldwide. The decipherment of hieroglyphs in the 19th century provided a key to unlocking the secrets of ancient Egyptian civilization. The study of hieroglyphs not only illuminated the history and culture of Egypt but also contributed to the understanding of other ancient writing systems and the evolution of human communication.

Egyptian mathematics also played a significant role in shaping the field of mathematics as we know it today. The Egyptians developed a decimal numerical system, used fractions, and possessed a deep understanding of geometry. Their mathematical knowledge influenced subsequent civilizations, including the Greeks, who built upon and expanded the foundations laid by the Egyptians.

Moreover, Egypt's cultural and religious practices, such as mummification and the worship of gods like Ra and Isis, captured the imagination of people worldwide. Egyptian art, with its iconic symbols and representations, has been a source of inspiration for artists, designers, and filmmakers throughout history.

In conclusion, Egypt's influence on the world is vast and enduring. Its architectural achievements, hieroglyphic writing system, mathematical contributions, and cultural practices have left an indelible mark on human civilization. By appreciating and studying Egypt's rich history and cultural heritage, we can continue to be inspired and learn from this ancient and remarkable civilization.

Day 2

- **Review your main idea and supporting details annotations from day 1.**
- **Answer all of the questions on the following pages.**

Which two of the following would make a great title for the text?

a. Egypt's Influence
b. Ancient Cities of Asia
c. Egypt's Influence on Greece
d. The Center of the World
e. The Beginning of Civilization
f. The Ancient City's Impact on Modern Times

Write your own title for the book.

_____

_____

_____

_____

_____

Questions

Who/what was the passage about?

_____

_____

What was the most important thing you learned about the "who"?

_____

_____

When does it take place?

_____

_____

Where does it take place?

_____

_____

Why/how does it happen?

_____

_____

In your own words, what is the main idea?

_____

_____

_____

_____

_____

_____

_____

_____

_____

_____

_____

_____

Which two details best support the main idea?

a. Egypt's influence helped to shape ancient cities like Mesopotamia and Greece.

b. Egypt's mathematics, culture, and architecture inspired many.

c. Modern times influenced Egypt's writing and math.

d. The pyrimids were a common structure in their day.

e. Egypt was an advanced civilization that had writing, math, and architecture.

f. Egypt was not very advanced.

Summarize the text in five sentences or less.

_____

_____

_____

_____

_____

_____

_____

_____

_____

_____

_____

_____

Main Idea Clue Chaser

- What is the title of the text? This is usually the main idea.
- You can also determine the main idea of a paragraph by reading the first sentence.
- The main idea can sometimes be found in the last sentence of a paragraph.
- You can find out the main idea of a text by synthesizing the main idea of each paragraph.
- Supporting details help to explain the main idea.
- The main idea is what the text is mostly about.
- The introduction paragraph likely explains the main idea, and supporting details of the text.
- Ask yourself what the text is mostly about.
- Think about the five W's of the passage to summarize the text or find the main idea:
  - Who is the text/paragraph about?
  - What did you learn about them?
  - When did the events take place?
  - Where did the events take place?
  - Why did the events take place?

Day 1

- As you read, underline the main idea of each paragraph and circle two supporting details in the same paragraph.

Food Chains and Food Webs: Interconnected Systems of Life

Food chains and food webs are intricate networks that depict the flow of energy and the interdependence of organisms in ecosystems. These concepts help us understand how energy is transferred from one organism to another, highlighting the delicate balance of nature.

A food chain is a linear representation of the transfer of energy through a series of organisms. It starts with producers, such as plants, which convert sunlight into food through photosynthesis. Herbivores, or primary consumers, feed on these plants, while carnivores and omnivores, known as secondary and tertiary consumers, respectively, prey on other animals. Decomposers, such as bacteria and fungi, break down dead organisms, returning nutrients to the soil.

However, in reality, ecosystems are much more complex than a simple linear chain. This complexity is captured in a food web, which depicts the interconnectedness of multiple food chains within an ecosystem. In a food web, organisms can occupy multiple roles, as they may eat and be eaten by various species. This interdependence ensures the stability and resilience of ecosystems, as disruptions in one part of the web can have cascading effects on other organisms.

Species at different trophic levels, or positions in the food chain, have specific roles and adaptations. Producers harness the sun's energy, while herbivores have adaptations to efficiently consume plant matter. Predators possess specialized traits for hunting and capturing prey, while decomposers play a vital role in breaking down organic matter and recycling nutrients.

Human activities can impact food chains and food webs, often leading to negative consequences. Habitat destruction, pollution, overfishing, and the introduction of invasive species can disrupt the delicate balance of ecosystems, causing species extinction and ecosystem degradation.

Understanding food chains and food webs is essential for ecological conservation and sustainable management of our natural resources. By recognizing the intricate connections and interdependencies among species, we can appreciate the importance of preserving biodiversity and maintaining the health of our ecosystems. Ultimately, a balanced and resilient web of life is essential for the survival and well-being of all organisms on our planet.

Day 2

- **Review your main idea and supporting details annotations from day 1.**
- **Answer all of the questions on the following pages.**

Which two of the following would make a great title for the text?

a. The food We Eat
b. Animals Hunt for Food
c. The Food Chains of Every Habitat
d. Food Chains and Food Webs
e. A Connected Nutrient Source
f. A Web of Spiders

Write your own title for the book.

_____

_____

_____

_____

_____

Questions

Quick Note: some of the questions below may not need to be filled out.
Complete this to the best of your ability.

Who/what was the passage about?

_____

_____

What was the most important thing you learned about the "who"?

_____

_____

When does it take place?

_____

_____

Where does it take place?

_____

_____

Why/how does it happen?

_____

_____

In your own words, what is the main idea?

_____

_____

_____

_____

_____

_____

_____

_____

_____

_____

_____

_____

_____

Which two details best support the main idea?

a. Plants are secondary producers.

b. Lions and Primary Producers.

c. A food web is a linear representation of the transfer of energy.

d. Food Chains and Webs are the same thing.

e. A food chain is a linear representation of the transfer of energy.

f. Food Chains and Webs show how animal recycle energy in the ecosystem.

Summarize the text in five sentences or less.

_____

_____

_____

_____

_____

_____

_____

_____

_____

_____

_____

_____

_____

Main Idea Clue Chaser

- What is the title of the text? This is usually the main idea.
- You can also determine the main idea of a paragraph by reading the first sentence.
- The main idea can sometimes be found in the last sentence of a paragraph.
- You can find out the main idea of a text by synthesizing the main idea of each paragraph.
- Supporting details help to explain the main idea.
- The main idea is what the text is mostly about.
- The introduction paragraph likely explains the main idea, and supporting details of the text.
- Ask yourself what the text is mostly about.
- Think about the five W's of the passage to summarize the text or find the main idea:
  - Who is the text/paragraph about?
  - What did you learn about them?
  - When did the events take place?
  - Where did the events take place?
  - Why did the events take place?

Day 2

- As you read, underline the main idea of each paragraph and circle two supporting details in the same paragraph.

The American Revolution: Birth of a Nation

The American Revolution, spanning from 1775 to 1783, marked a turning point in the history of the United States and had far-reaching implications for the world. It was a struggle for independence from British colonial rule and a quest for self-governance that ultimately led to the birth of a new nation.

Tensions between the American colonies and the British Empire had been simmering for years, fueled by issues such as taxation without representation and a desire for greater autonomy. The revolutionary fervor gained momentum with events like the Boston Tea Party in 1773, where colonists protested against British tea taxes by dumping chests of tea into the harbor.

The conflict escalated into open warfare in 1775 with the battles of Lexington and Concord, often considered the start of the Revolution. The Continental Congress, representing the thirteen colonies, declared independence on July 4, 1776, with the adoption of the Declaration of Independence, a powerful document asserting the inherent rights of individuals and the legitimacy of self-governance.

The Revolution was fought on multiple fronts, with iconic battles such as the Battle of Bunker Hill, Saratoga, and Yorktown. The American forces, led by General George Washington, faced significant challenges but managed to secure crucial victories, aided by alliances with nations like France.

The Treaty of Paris in 1783 formally ended the Revolutionary War, recognizing the United States as an independent nation. The Revolution's legacy was profound, establishing the principles of individual liberty, representative government, and the pursuit of happiness that became the foundation of American democracy. The American Revolution inspired subsequent independence movements around the world, shaping the course of history. It laid the groundwork for the U.S. Constitution, adopted in 1787, and influenced the development of democratic principles globally.

Today, the American Revolution stands as a testament to the enduring spirit of freedom and the power of a people's collective will to determine their own destiny. It continues to be celebrated as a defining moment in American history, reminding us of the importance of liberty and the ongoing pursuit of a more perfect union.

Day 2

- Review your main idea and supporting details annotations from day 1.
- Answer all of the questions on the following pages.

Which two of the following would make a great title for the text?

a. The Greatest War
b. The Revolution
c. The United Kingdom's Freedom
d. America vs the World
e. The American Revolution
f. Taxation Without Representation

Write your own title for the book.

_____

_____

_____

_____

_____

_____

Questions

Quick Note: some of the questions below may not need to be filled out.
Complete this to the best of your ability.

Who/what was the passage about?

_____

_____

What was the most important thing you learned about the "who"?

_____

_____

When does it take place?

_____

_____

Where does it take place?

_____

_____

Why/how does it happen?

_____

_____

In your own words, what is the main idea?

_____

_____

_____

_____

_____

_____

_____

_____

_____

_____

_____

_____

_____

Which two details best support the main idea?

a. The American Revolution did not effect the lives of americans very much.

b. The American Revolution lead to several wars that ended in 1923.

c. The American Revolution lead to the formation of the United Kingdom.

d. The American Revolution marked a turning point in the history of the United States.

e. The American Revolution started because of a dispute over unfair tax laws.

f. The American revolution ended when the Brittish won the war in 1855.

Summarize the text in five sentences or less.

_____

_____

_____

_____

_____

_____

_____

_____

_____

_____

_____

_____

_____

_____

Main Idea Clue Chaser

- What is the title of the text? This is usually the main idea.
- You can also determine the main idea of a paragraph by reading the first sentence.
- The main idea can sometimes be found in the last sentence of a paragraph.
- You can find out the main idea of a text by synthesizing the main idea of each paragraph.
- Supporting details help to explain the main idea.
- The main idea is what the text is mostly about.
- The introduction paragraph likely explains the main idea, and supporting details of the text.
- Ask yourself what the text is mostly about.
- Think about the five W's of the passage to summarize the text or find the main idea:
  - Who is the text/paragraph about?
  - What did you learn about them?
  - When did the events take place?
  - Where did the events take place?
  - Why did the events take place?

Day

- As you read, underline the main idea of each paragraph and circle two supporting details in the same paragraph.

Nelson Mandela: A Global Icon of Freedom and Reconciliation

Nelson Mandela, the revered leader and symbol of the anti-apartheid movement in South Africa, left an indelible impact not only on his country but also on the world. Through his unwavering commitment to justice, reconciliation, and equality, Mandela's influence transcended borders, inspiring generations and transforming societies.

Mandela's journey to dismantling apartheid began long before his presidency. As a young activist, he co-founded the African National Congress Youth League, advocating for equal rights and opposing the oppressive policies of the apartheid government. His unwavering dedication to the cause of freedom led to his imprisonment in 1962, where he spent 27 years incarcerated.

Upon his release in 1990, Mandela emerged as a unifying figure, leading negotiations with the apartheid government and steering South Africa toward democracy. His presidency from 1994 to 1999 was marked by his commitment to reconciliation and nation-building. Mandela established the Truth and Reconciliation Commission, a groundbreaking initiative that aimed to heal the wounds of the past through a process of truth-telling and forgiveness.

Mandela's impact extended far beyond the borders of South Africa. He became a global advocate for human rights, social justice, and peace. His unwavering belief in the power of dialogue and understanding resonated with people worldwide, inspiring movements for freedom and justice across continents.

Mandela's legacy of leadership and resilience continues to shape South Africa. His vision of a united, non-racial, and democratic society remains an ongoing aspiration for the nation. The values he embodied—forgiveness, inclusivity, and the pursuit of equality—serve as guiding principles for a more just and equitable world.

Nelson Mandela's impact reaches beyond his presidency and his passing in 2013. His life and teachings continue to inspire individuals and movements committed to fighting discrimination, oppression, and injustice. Mandela's unwavering commitment to freedom and equality stands as a testament to the enduring power of compassion, forgiveness, and the belief that individuals can make a difference in shaping a better world for all.

Day 2

- Review your main idea and supporting details annotations from day 1.
- Answer all of the questions on the following pages.

Which three of the following would make a great title for the text?

a. The History of South Africa
b. The Road to Freedom in Africa
c. West African Independence
d. President Mandela
e. Mandela's impact on South Africa
f. The Influence of Mandela

Write your own title for the book.

_____

_____

_____

_____

_____

Questions

Quick Note: some of the questions below may not need to be filled out.
Complete this to the best of your ability.

Who/what was the passage about?

_____

_____

What was the most important thing you learned about the "who"?

_____

_____

When does it take place?

_____

_____

Where does it take place?

_____

_____

Why/how does it happen?

_____

_____

In your own words, what is the main idea?

_____

_____

_____

_____

_____

_____

_____

_____

_____

_____

_____

_____

_____

Which two details best support the main idea?

a. Mandela's legacy of leadership and resilience continues to shape South Africa.

b. Nelson Mandela's impact reaches beyond his presidency

c. Mandela's impact in America was vast.

d. South Africa was the last country to be freed in 1999.

e. Nelson Mandela fought for freedom in Sudan.

f. The South America Revolution happened at the end of apartheid.

Summarize the text in five sentences or less.

_____

_____

_____

_____

_____

_____

_____

_____

_____

_____

_____

_____

_____

Main Idea Clue Chaser

- What is the title of the text? This is usually the main idea.
- You can also determine the main idea of a paragraph by reading the first sentence.
- The main idea can sometimes be found in the last sentence of a paragraph.
- You can find out the main idea of a text by synthesizing the main idea of each paragraph.
- Supporting details help to explain the main idea.
- The main idea is what the text is mostly about.
- The introduction paragraph likely explains the main idea, and supporting details of the text.
- Ask yourself what the text is mostly about.
- Think about the five W's of the passage to summarize the text or find the main idea:
  - Who is the text/paragraph about?
  - What did you learn about them?
  - When did the events take place?
  - Where did the events take place?
  - Why did the events take place?

Day 1

- As you read, underline the main idea of each paragraph and circle two supporting details in the same paragraph.

Mansa Musa: The Golden King of Mali

Mansa Musa, also known as Musa of Mali, was a legendary figure who reigned over the Mali Empire in West Africa during the 14th century. His wealth, influence, and cultural impact made him one of the most remarkable rulers in history.

Mansa Musa's reign coincided with a period of great prosperity for the Mali Empire, which controlled vast territories and was a hub of trade and commerce. What set Mansa Musa apart was his immense wealth, primarily derived from the empire's vast gold reserves. His empire was the largest producer of gold in the world, and Mansa Musa's personal wealth was said to be unrivaled. His legendary pilgrimage to Mecca in 1324 further solidified his reputation and brought him to the attention of the wider world.

Mansa Musa's pilgrimage to Mecca showcased his wealth and generosity. His caravan consisted of thousands of people, including soldiers, scholars, and merchants, along with an entourage of servants carrying gold and precious gifts. During his journey, Mansa Musa distributed vast amounts of gold, giving alms to the poor and leaving a trail of awe and wonder wherever he went. His generosity and lavish spending inadvertently caused a temporary decline in the value of gold in the regions he visited.

Beyond his immense wealth, Mansa Musa was a devout Muslim and a patron of education and the arts. He commissioned the construction of grand mosques, schools, and libraries, fostering a climate of intellectual and cultural growth within the empire. Timbuktu, a city within the Mali Empire, became a renowned center of learning and scholarship under his patronage.

Mansa Musa's impact extended beyond his reign and his empire. His pilgrimage and the stories of his wealth and generosity spread far and wide, drawing attention to West Africa and its rich resources. His reign and legacy solidified the Mali Empire's reputation as a powerful and influential force in the medieval world.

In conclusion, Mansa Musa's legacy as the Golden King of Mali is one of immense wealth, cultural patronage, and religious devotion. His reign showcased the economic power of the Mali Empire and brought international attention to West Africa. Mansa Musa's story continues to inspire and captivate, serving as a testament to the greatness that can be achieved through leadership, wealth, and a commitment to the betterment of one's people.

Day 2

- **Review your main idea and supporting details annotations from day 1.**
- **Answer all of the questions on the following pages.**

Which three of the following would make a great title for the text?

a. The King of Gold in Africa
b. The Golden King of Egypt
c. The Royal Family in Africa
d. President of the South Africans
e. Currency, Culture, and Electronics
f. Musa of Mali

Write your own title for the book.

_____

_____

_____

_____

_____

_____

Questions

Quick Note: some of the questions below may not need to be filled out.
Complete this to the best of your ability.

Who/what was the passage about?

_____

_____

What was the most important thing you learned about the "who"?

_____

_____

When does it take place?

_____

_____

Where does it take place?

_____

_____

Why/how does it happen?

_____

_____

In your own words, what is the main idea?

_____

_____

_____

_____

_____

_____

_____

_____

_____

_____

_____

_____

Which two details best support the main idea?

a. Mansa Musa did not like the arts and banned them from his country.

b. His pilgrimage and the stories of his wealth and generosity spread far and wide, drawing attention to West Africa and its rich resources.

c. Beyond his immense wealth, Mansa Musa was a devout Muslim and a patron of education and the arts.

d. Musa did not travel anywhere in his lifetime.

e. Mansa Musa reigned over the Mali Empire in West Africa during the 14th century.

Summarize the text in five sentences or less.

_____

_____

_____

_____

_____

_____

_____

_____

_____

_____

_____

_____

_____

_____

Main Idea Clue Chaser

- What is the title of the text? This is usually the main idea.
- You can also determine the main idea of a paragraph by reading the first sentence.
- The main idea can sometimes be found in the last sentence of a paragraph.
- You can find out the main idea of a text by synthesizing the main idea of each paragraph.
- Supporting details help to explain the main idea.
- The main idea is what the text is mostly about.
- The introduction paragraph likely explains the main idea, and supporting details of the text.
- Ask yourself what the text is mostly about.
- Think about the five W's of the passage to summarize the text or find the main idea:
  - Who is the text/paragraph about?
  - What did you learn about them?
  - When did the events take place?
  - Where did the events take place?
  - Why did the events take place?

Day 1

- As you read, underline the main idea of each paragraph and circle two supporting details in the same paragraph.

Our Solar System: A Celestial Neighborhood

The solar system is a vast and awe-inspiring expanse of celestial bodies that orbits around our central star, the Sun. It consists of eight planets, numerous moons, asteroids, comets, and other smaller objects. Understanding the solar system helps us appreciate the incredible diversity and complexity of our cosmic neighborhood.

At the heart of our solar system is the Sun, a massive ball of hot gas that provides the light, heat, and energy necessary for life on Earth. The Sun's gravitational pull holds the solar system together, while its nuclear reactions generate the vast amount of energy radiated into space. Mercury, Venus, Earth, and Mars are the four rocky inner planets, known as the terrestrial planets, which are relatively small and composed primarily of rock and metal. Beyond Mars lies the asteroid belt, a region populated by numerous rocky and metallic fragments.

Jupiter, Saturn, Uranus, and Neptune are the gas giants, or outer planets, composed primarily of hydrogen and helium. These giants are much larger than the terrestrial planets and possess massive atmospheres and ring systems. Jupiter, the largest planet, has a complex weather system and a conspicuous Great Red Spot—a persistent storm.

Moons, natural satellites that orbit planets, are also an essential part of the solar system. Earth has one moon, while Jupiter and Saturn boast the most extensive moon systems, with dozens each. Some moons, like Jupiter's Europa and Saturn's Titan, have environments that may harbor the conditions necessary for life.

Comets and asteroids, remnants from the early solar system, orbit the Sun in various trajectories. Comets are icy bodies that originate in the outer regions of the solar system and develop a glowing coma and tail as they approach the Sun. Asteroids, rocky objects primarily found in the asteroid belt, range in size from small boulders to dwarf planets like Ceres.

Studying the solar system provides insights into the formation and evolution of planets, the potential for life beyond Earth, and our place in the universe. Space missions, telescopic observations, and scientific research continue to deepen our understanding of the solar system and ignite our curiosity about the mysteries of the cosmos.

In conclusion, our solar system is a mesmerizing tapestry of planets, moons, asteroids, comets, and other celestial objects. From the scorching inner planets to the majestic gas giants, the diversity and grandeur of our solar system inspire wonder and encourage exploration. By studying and appreciating this celestial neighborhood, we gain a deeper understanding of the universe and our place within it.

Day 2

- Review your main idea and supporting details annotations from day 1.
- Answer all of the questions on the following pages.

Which three of the following would make a great title for the text?

a. Our Star, Our Planets
b. The Life Supporting Systems of Earth
c. The Gas Giants of Our Solar System
d. The Solar system
e. The Rocks of Mars
f. The Way Our Planet Works

Write your own title for the book.

_____

_____

_____

_____

_____

Questions

Quick Note: some of the questions below may not need to be filled out.
Complete this to the best of your ability.

Who/what was the passage about?

_____

_____

What was the most important thing you learned about the "who"?

_____

_____

When does it take place?

_____

_____

Where does it take place?

_____

_____

Why/how does it happen?

_____

_____

In your own words, what is the main idea?

_____

_____

_____

_____

_____

_____

_____

_____

_____

_____

_____

_____

Which two details best support the main idea?

a. The rocks on Mars are similar to the rocks on Earth.

b. Jupiter, Saturn, Uranus, and Neptune are gas giants.

c. Scientist have found water on Mars.

d. Scientists have not found intelligent life on other plants.

e. Moons are natural satellites that orbit planets.

f. The earth has two moons. One moon shaped like a circle, and another shaped like a crescent.

Summarize the text in five sentences or less.

_____

_____

_____

_____

_____

_____

_____

_____

_____

_____

_____

_____

_____

_____

Main Idea Clue Chaser

- What is the title of the text? This is usually the main idea.
- You can also determine the main idea of a paragraph by reading the first sentence.
- The main idea can sometimes be found in the last sentence of a paragraph.
- You can find out the main idea of a text by synthesizing the main idea of each paragraph.
- Supporting details help to explain the main idea.
- The main idea is what the text is mostly about.
- The introduction paragraph likely explains the main idea, and supporting details of the text.
- Ask yourself what the text is mostly about.
- Think about the five W's of the passage to summarize the text or find the main idea:
  - Who is the text/paragraph about?
  - What did you learn about them?
  - When did the events take place?
  - Where did the events take place?
  - Why did the events take place?

Day 1

- As you read, underline the main idea of each paragraph and circle two supporting details in the same paragraph.

Electromagnetism: Powering Modern Life

Electromagnetism, the science that explores the relationship between electricity and magnetism, plays a pivotal role in shaping our modern world. From the simplest gadgets to complex technologies, our daily lives are heavily reliant on the principles and applications of electromagnetism.

One of the most notable impacts of electromagnetism is the generation and distribution of electricity. The ability to produce electric power through generators and harness it for various purposes revolutionized society. Electricity powers our homes, industries, transportation systems, and communication networks. It enables us to light our homes, run appliances, charge our devices, and access the vast realm of information on the internet.

Electromagnetic waves, such as radio waves, microwaves, infrared, visible light, ultraviolet, X-rays, and gamma rays, have become indispensable in communication and information technologies. Radio waves allow for wireless communication, including broadcasting, cellular networks, and Wi-Fi. Microwaves enable us to heat food quickly and efficiently. Infrared technology finds applications in remote controls, thermal imaging, and security systems.

Visible light is essential for vision and optical technologies. X-rays and gamma rays are used in medical diagnostics and treatments.

The development of electromechanical devices has transformed various industries. Electric motors power machinery, vehicles, and appliances, making them more efficient and reliable. Electromagnetic sensors and actuators are integrated into a wide range of systems, from automotive and aerospace to robotics and automation, enhancing functionality and control. Furthermore, electromagnetism underpins the field of electronics. Transistors, integrated circuits, and computer chips form the foundation of modern electronics, allowing us to create powerful computers, smartphones, and other electronic devices that have become an integral part of our lives.

While electromagnetism has undoubtedly brought immense benefits, it also presents challenges. Electromagnetic interference can disrupt electronic systems, leading to communication failures or malfunctions. Safeguarding against such interference and minimizing its effects require careful engineering and design.

In conclusion, the impact of electromagnetism on modern

life is profound and far-reaching. From the generation and distribution of electricity to communication technologies, electromagnetism powers our homes, fuels innovation, and enables global connectivity. Our ability to harness and understand electromagnetism has revolutionized industries, transformed the way we live and work, and opened up new realms of possibility for future advancements.

Day 2

- **Review your main idea and supporting details annotations from day 1.**
- **Answer all of the questions on the following pages.**

Which three of the following would make a great title for the text?

a. Our Planet
b. The Earth's Electromagnetic Poles
c. The Sun's EMF Waves
d. Electromagnetic Waves
e. Magnets, Electricity, and You
f. Magnets, Rain, and Power

Write your own title for the book.

_____

_____

_____

_____

_____

Questions

Quick Note: some of the questions below may not need to be filled out.
Complete this to the best of your ability.

Who/what was the passage about?

_____

_____

What was the most important thing you learned about the "who"?

_____

_____

When does it take place?

_____

_____

Where does it take place?

_____

_____

Why/how does it happen?

_____

_____

In your own words, what is the main idea?

_____

_____

_____

_____

_____

_____

_____

_____

_____

_____

_____

_____

Which two details best support the main idea?

a. Magnetism and Electricity are the same in space.

b. Electric motors power machinery, vehicles, and appliances, making them more efficient and reliable

c. One impact of electromagnetism is the generation and distribution of electricity.

d. Scientists have not found intelligent life on other plants.

e. Electromagnetic energy can not be used to power cars.

f. Electromagnetic energy is generated in the earth's poles.

Summarize the text in five sentences or less.

_____

_____

_____

_____

_____

_____

_____

_____

_____

_____

_____

_____

_____

_____

Main Idea Clue Chaser

- What is the title of the text? This is usually the main idea.
- You can also determine the main idea of a paragraph by reading the first sentence.
- The main idea can sometimes be found in the last sentence of a paragraph.
- You can find out the main idea of a text by synthesizing the main idea of each paragraph.
- Supporting details help to explain the main idea.
- The main idea is what the text is mostly about.
- The introduction paragraph likely explains the main idea, and supporting details of the text.
- Ask yourself what the text is mostly about.
- Think about the five W's of the passage to summarize the text or find the main idea:
  - Who is the text/paragraph about?
  - What did you learn about them?
  - When did the events take place?
  - Where did the events take place?
  - Why did the events take place?

Day 1

- As you read, underline the main idea of each paragraph and circle two supporting details in the same paragraph.

The Water Cycle: Nature's Endless Circulation

The water cycle, also known as the hydrological cycle, is a continuous process through which water circulates between the Earth's surface, the atmosphere, and back again. It is a vital natural phenomenon that ensures the availability of water for all life forms on our planet.

The water cycle begins with evaporation. Heat from the Sun causes water bodies, such as oceans, lakes, and rivers, to convert into water vapor, a gaseous state. This vapor rises into the atmosphere, forming clouds through a process called condensation. As the water vapor cools, it transforms back into tiny water droplets that gather together to create visible clouds.

Next comes precipitation. When the water droplets in the clouds grow too heavy, they fall back to the Earth's surface in the form of rain, snow, sleet, or hail. Precipitation replenishes water sources on land, including rivers, lakes, and groundwater, ensuring the availability of freshwater for plants, animals, and humans.

Once on the ground, water follows various paths. Some of it may be absorbed into the soil, becoming part of the groundwater system. From there, it can slowly seep into rivers, lakes, and oceans, completing the cycle.

Alternatively, water on the land surface can flow into streams and rivers, eventually reaching the ocean. This movement of water on the Earth's surface is called runoff.

The water cycle is a dynamic process that affects weather patterns and regulates the Earth's climate. It plays a critical role in distributing heat energy across the globe, influencing temperature variations and driving atmospheric circulation. Additionally, the water cycle contributes to the formation of clouds, which help regulate the amount of sunlight reaching the Earth's surface.

Understanding the water cycle is essential for managing and conserving water resources. It helps scientists and policymakers develop strategies to address water scarcity, droughts, floods, and other water-related challenges. It also highlights the interconnectedness of different ecosystems and emphasizes the need for sustainable water management practices.

In conclusion, the water cycle is a continuous and essential process that ensures the distribution and availability of water on Earth. From evaporation and condensation to precipitation and runoff, this cycle facilitates the replenishment of water sources, regulates climate, and sustains life. Appreciating the water cycle enables us to appreciate the interconnectedness of Earth's systems and the importance of responsible water management for the well-being of our planet.

Day 2

- Review your main idea and supporting details annotations from day 1.
- Answer all of the questions on the following pages.

Which three of the following would make a great title for the text?

a. Earth's Water

b. Evaporation, Precipitation, Circulation

c. Rain

d. Earth's Water Cycle

e. The Sun's Influence on the Water Cycle

f. The Water Cycle of Mars

Write your own title for the book.

_____

_____

_____

_____

_____

Questions

Quick Note: some of the questions below may not need to be filled out.
Complete this to the best of your ability.

Who/what was the passage about?

_____

_____

What was the most important thing you learned about the "who"?

_____

_____

When does it take place?

_____

_____

Where does it take place?

_____

_____

Why/how does it happen?

_____

_____

In your own words, what is the main idea?

_____

_____

_____

_____

_____

_____

_____

_____

_____

_____

_____

_____

_____

Which three details best support the main idea?

a. Water Originally came from a comet that fell to earth from spcace.

b. Next comes precipitation. When the water droplets in the clouds grow too heavy.

c. The water cycle begins with evaporation.

d. Scientists still do no fully understand the water cycle.

e. Clouds do not effect the water cycle.

Summarize the text in five sentences or less.

_____

_____

_____

_____

_____

_____

_____

_____

_____

_____

_____

_____

_____

Main Idea Clue Chaser

- What is the title of the text? This is usually the main idea.
- You can also determine the main idea of a paragraph by reading the first sentence.
- The main idea can sometimes be found in the last sentence of a paragraph.
- You can find out the main idea of a text by synthesizing the main idea of each paragraph.
- Supporting details help to explain the main idea.
- The main idea is what the text is mostly about.
- The introduction paragraph likely explains the main idea, and supporting details of the text.
- Ask yourself what the text is mostly about.
- Think about the five W's of the passage to summarize the text or find the main idea:
    - Who is the text/paragraph about?
    - What did you learn about them?
    - When did the events take place?
    - Where did the events take place?
    - Why did the events take place?

Day 1

- As you read, underline the main idea of each paragraph and circle two supporting details in the same paragraph.

The Importance of Renewable Sources of Energy: A Sustainable Future

Renewable sources of energy are becoming increasingly vital in our quest for a sustainable future. Unlike fossil fuels, which are finite and contribute to environmental degradation, renewable energy offers a clean, abundant, and inexhaustible alternative. Harnessing the power of renewable sources has numerous benefits, from reducing greenhouse gas emissions to promoting energy independence and fostering economic growth.

One of the primary advantages of renewable energy is its environmental impact. Unlike fossil fuels, renewable sources such as solar, wind, hydro, and geothermal energy produce little to no greenhouse gas emissions, which are major contributors to climate change. By transitioning to renewable energy, we can mitigate the negative effects of carbon emissions, decrease air pollution, and preserve our natural environment.

Renewable energy also helps reduce our reliance on finite fossil fuel reserves, promoting energy independence. As renewable sources are widely available and can be harnessed locally, countries can reduce their dependence on imported fuels, enhancing energy security. This diversification of energy sources reduces vulnerability to price fluctuations and geopolitical tensions, fostering greater stability and resilience.

Furthermore, the adoption of renewable energy technologies drives economic growth and job creation. The renewable energy sector is a rapidly expanding industry, providing employment opportunities across various fields, including manufacturing, installation, maintenance, and research. Investing in renewable energy infrastructure stimulates local economies, attracts investment, and fosters innovation, leading to long-term economic benefits.

Renewable energy also brings energy access to remote and underdeveloped regions. In areas without access to centralized power grids, off-grid renewable solutions, such as solar panels and small-scale wind turbines, provide reliable electricity for households, schools, and healthcare facilities. This improves quality of life, supports education and economic development, and reduces reliance on expensive and polluting alternatives like diesel generators.

In conclusion, the importance of renewable sources of energy cannot be overstated. By transitioning to clean and sustainable energy systems, we can mitigate climate change, reduce pollution, enhance energy security, and drive economic growth. Embracing renewable energy technologies is not just an environmental imperative, but also an opportunity to create a more resilient and prosperous future for generations to come.

Day 2

- Review your main idea and supporting details annotations from day 1.
- Answer all of the questions on the following pages.

Which one of the titles below fits the text.

a. Wind Power
b. Solar Power
c. Fossil Fuels
d. A Sustainable Future

Write your own title for the book.

_____

_____

_____

_____

_____

Questions

Quick Note: some of the questions below may not need to be filled out.
Complete this to the best of your ability.

Who/what was the passage about?

_____

_____

What was the most important thing you learned about the "who"?

_____

_____

When does it take place?

_____

_____

Where does it take place?

_____

_____

Why/how does it happen?

_____

_____

In your own words, what is the main idea?

_____

_____

_____

_____

_____

_____

_____

_____

_____

_____

_____

_____

_____

Which detail best support the main idea?

a. Renewable sources of energy are becoming increasingly vital

b. Renewable energy will not be available until twenty years in the future.

c. It is impossible for energy to be entirely renewable..

d. Scientists still do not understand renewable energy..

Summarize the text in five sentences or less.

_____

_____

_____

_____

_____

_____

_____

_____

_____

_____

_____

_____

_____

★★★★★

PLEASE CONSIDER LEAVING A REVIEW ON
AMAZON IF YOU LIKED THIS BOOK!